W9-CII-421

WOULD YOU DARE
GO
SKYDIVING?

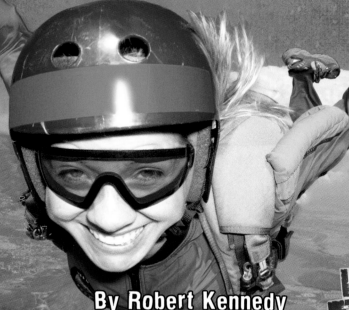

By Robert Kennedy

HOT TOPICS

Gareth Stevens
PUBLISHING

Please visit our website, www.garethstevens.com. For a free color catalog of all our high-quality books, call toll free 1-800-542-2595 or fax 1-877-542-2596.

Cataloging-in-Publication Data

Names: Kennedy, Robert.
Title: Would you dare go skydiving? / Robert Kennedy.
Description: New York : Gareth Stevens, 2017. | Series: Would you dare? | Includes index.
Identifiers: ISBN 9781482458183 (pbk.) | ISBN 9781482458206 (library bound) | ISBN 9781482458190 (6 pack)
Subjects: LCSH: Skydiving--Juvenile literature.
Classification: LCC GV770.K46 2017 | DDC 797.56--dc23

First Edition

Published in 2017 by
Gareth Stevens Publishing
111 East 14th Street, Suite 349
New York, NY 10003

Designer: Laura Bowen
Editor: Therese Shea

Photo credits: Cover, p. 1 (skydiver) Joel Kiesel/Stone/Getty Images; cover, p. 1 (plane) Nadeza Murmakova/Shutterstock.com; cover, pp. 1–32 (background) Nik Merkulov/Shutterstock.com; cover, pp. 1–32 (paint splat) Milan M/Shutterstock.com; cover, pp. 1–32 (photo frame) Milos Djapovic/Shutterstock.com; p. 5 Mauricio Graiki/Shutterstock.com; pp. 7, 14, 22, 23 Sindre T/Shutterstock.com; p. 8 Deymos.HR/Shutterstock.com; p. 9 FlavioAlmeida/Moment Open/Getty Images; p. 11 dzphotovideo/E+/Getty Images; pp. 13, 24, 26, 30 Germanskydiver/Shutterstock.com; p. 15 Antonio Nardelli/Shutterstock.com; p. 17 Darryl Leniuk/Digital Vision/Getty Images; p. 19 Aleksei Lazukov/Shutterstock.com; pp. 21, 27 Rick Neves/Moment/Getty Images; p. 25 (top) Matanya/Wikimedia Commons; p. 25 (bottom) Spellcast/Wikimedia Commons; p. 29 bikeriderlondon/Shutterstock.com.

Printed in the United States of America

CPSIA compliance information: Batch #CW17GS: For further information contact Gareth Stevens, New York, New York at 1-800-542-2595.

CONTENTS

READY TO JUMP?

You're 8,000 feet (2,438 m) above the ground. The door to the plane is open. You can't see much on the ground. It looks like pieces of a quilt! The skydiving instructor asks if you're ready to jump. Do you dare?

DARING DATA

"Acrophobia" is the great fear of heights. You'd better not be acrophobic if you're going to skydive!

DON'T FORGET THE PARACHUTE!

Skydiving is an activity in which people jump from an airplane or other surface, usually 7,500 to 15,000 feet (2,286 to 4,572 m) in the air. They fall and then open a **parachute** to slow down and reach the ground safely.

DARING DATA

Frenchman André-Jacques Garnerin first jumped from an air balloon with a parachute in 1797. In 1911, Grant Morton jumped from a plane in California.

Jumping and opening a parachute may sound easy, but skydiving takes a lot of preparation. Skydivers wear special jumpsuits. They also wear a special rig. It's a kind of backpack that holds two parachutes. One parachute is in case the other doesn't work!

rig

DARING DATA

An even smaller parachute called the pilot chute comes
out of the rig first. It catches the wind and makes
the parachute called the main canopy **inflate**.

9

Falling in the air before the parachute comes out is called free fall. How long a skydiver free-falls depends on many things, including the **altitude** of the plane and wind speed. At 9,000 feet (2,743 m), skydivers free-fall for about 30 seconds.

DARING DATA

If a parachute is deployed, or used, at around 5,000 feet (1,524 m), the skydiver has about 4 minutes to enjoy the view before touching ground!

SPEED TALK

How fast a skydiver falls depends on weight, clothing, and position. For example, many fall "belly down." Divers usually free-fall at about 120 miles (193 km) per hour. In **competitions**, a jumper diving headfirst may reach speeds of more than 300 miles (483 km) per hour.

DARING DATA

An AAD (Automatic Activation Device) will open the
parachute in case the jumper gets too close to the
ground without opening it. It's another tool in the rig.

13

Some skydivers say the feeling of falling is like being on top of a pillow of air! When the main parachute opens, the skydiver's speed slows to about 10 miles (16 km) per hour. Landings are usually gentle.

DARING DATA

Safe skydiving drop zones don't have **obstacles**, such as trees, in the way of a landing.

15

DIVE
BUDDIES

Don't worry—you don't have to skydive alone the first time. You'll probably go tandem. That means a student skydiver is connected to a teacher, sometimes called a jumpmaster. The jumpmaster wears the parachute rig and makes sure the parachute deploys.

DARING DATA

Jumpmasters may do special turns and flips in the air!

AFF

When you're ready to skydive by yourself, you can take accelerated freefall (AFF) classes. Jumpers need several hours of ground instruction before they start jumping. Classes show you how to pack a rig, exit the aircraft, and position the body during free fall.

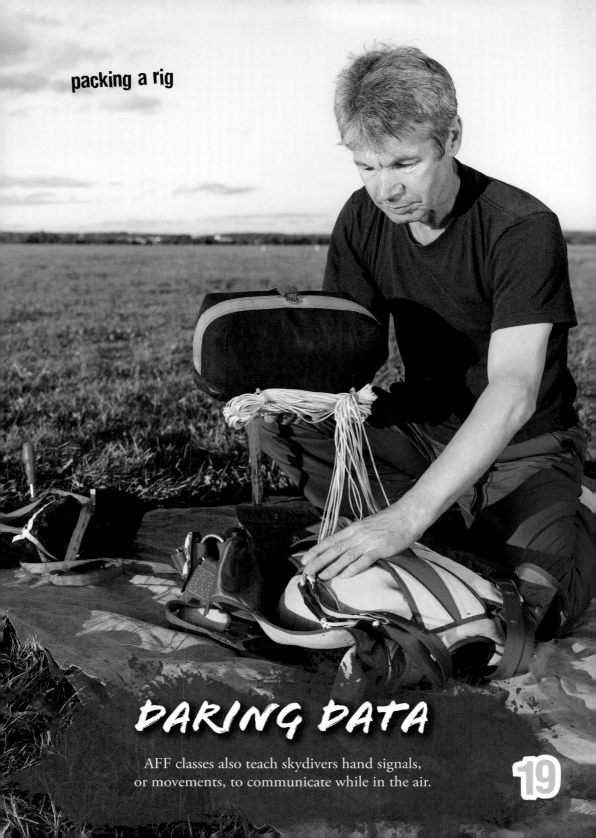

DARING DATA

AFF classes also teach skydivers hand signals,
or movements, to communicate while in the air.

During AFF training, two instructors jump with a student and tell them how to move through the whole dive. They use hand signals and radios during the fall and hold on to the student until parachute deployment.

DARING DATA

AFF students open their own parachute, often by pulling a rip cord.

21

The United States Parachute Association AFF program is seven levels. By the third level, students free-fall by themselves. Upper levels teach students how to make turns in the air, "dock" on other divers, and other skills.

DARING DATA

Each AFF level requires about 45 minutes of training.

23

After successfully completing a jump for each AFF level, a skydiving student goes to the next level. After completing Level 7, the student can still improve. However, they work with a coach to improve their skills at this point.

line training in
the US Army

DARING DATA

In static line training, a line connects skydivers
to an aircraft. The line pulls the parachute open
until the student is ready to do so.

LICENSE TO JUMP

After at least 25 successful jumps, a skydiver can get their USPA A **license**. They then can jump wherever they want. They can go on to earn B, C, and D licenses as their skill level increases.

DARING DATA

After earning an A license, a skydiver is no longer a student!

ARE YOU READY?

Skilled skydivers may enter competitions alone. They may have to land on a small **target**. They may enter a group competition and make amazing formations in the sky! Skydiving is a growing sport. So, would you dare make the jump?

DARING DATA

BASE jumping is when someone with a parachute jumps from a very high point, such as a building, bridge, or cliff, rather than an airplane. It's very dangerous.

29

USPA SAFETY

Here are some safety tips from the USPA:

- Land with your feet and knees together to avoid harm.

- Land in a clear area.

- Before each jump, review methods to avoid and handle emergency events.

- The smallest aircraft for student jumping should be able to carry the pilot and at least three jumpers.

- Skydivers need to know how to choose a correct exit point and guide the pilot to a clear landing area.

- Parachutes should not be rented or loaned to skydivers of unknown ability.

FOR MORE INFORMATION

BOOKS

Bailey, Diane. *Skydiving*. Vero Beach, FL: Rourke Educational Media, 2015.

Loh-Hagan, Virginia. *Extreme Sky Diving*. Ann Arbor, MI: Cherry Lake Publishing, 2016.

McFee, Shane. *Skydiving*. New York, NY: PowerKids Press, 2008.

WEBSITES

How Skydiving Works
adventure.howstuffworks.com/skydiving4.htm
See step-by-step photos of how the parachute system works.

USPA
www.uspa.org
The USPA site has everything you need to know about skydiving.

GLOSSARY

altitude: the height of an airplane above the level of the sea

competition: the act or process of trying to win something

emergency: an unexpected and usually dangerous event that calls for quick action

inflate: to become larger by being filled with air or gas

license: official permission to do something

obstacle: something that blocks your path

parachute: a piece of gear usually made of cloth that is fastened to people and allows them to fall slowly and land safely after they have jumped from an aircraft

target: a place or object at which to aim

INDEX